THE *Skinny*

BLEND ▶ *ACTIVE*

& PERSONAL BLENDER RECIPE BOOK

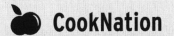

CookNation

THE SKINNY BLEND ACTIVE & PERSONAL BLENDER RECIPE BOOK

GREAT TASTING, NUTRITIOUS SMOOTHIES, JUICES & SHAKES. PERFECT FOR WORKOUTS, WEIGHT LOSS & FAT BURNING. BLEND & GO!

ISBN 978-1-910771-12-9

A CIP catalogue record of this book is available from the British Library

DISCLAIMER

This book is designed to provide information on smoothies and juices that can be made in the Breville Blend Active and other personal blender appliances, results may differ if alternative devices are used.

BREVILLE is a trademark of Breville Pty Ltd. Bell & Mackenzie Publishing is not affiliated with the owner of the trademark and is not an authorized distributor of the trademark owner's products or services. This publication has not been prepared, approved, or licensed by Breville Pty.

Breville were not involved in the recipe development or testing of any of the recipes on this book.

Some recipes may contain nuts or traces of nuts. Those suffering from any allergies associated with nuts should avoid any recipes containing nuts or nut based oils.

This information is provided and sold with the knowledge that the publisher and author do not offer any legal or other professional advice.

In the case of a need for any such expertise consult with the appropriate professional.

This book does not contain all information available on the subject, and other sources of recipes are available.

This book has not been created to be specific to any individual's or Breville's requirements.

Every effort has been made to make this book as accurate as possible. However, there may be typographical and or content errors. Therefore, this book should serve only as a general guide and not as the ultimate source of subject information.

This book contains information that might be dated and is intended only to educate and entertain.

The author and publisher shall have no liability or responsibility to any person or entity regarding any loss or damage incurred, or alleged to have incurred, directly or indirectly, by the information contained in this book.

CONTENTS

UNDER 400 CALORIES

You may also enjoy.....

DELICIOUS, NUTRITIOUS & SUPER-FAST MEALS IN 15 MINUTES OR LESS. ALL UNDER 300, 400 & 500 CALORIES

ISBN 978-1-909855-42-7

SIMPLE & DELICIOUS, FUSS FREE, FAST DAY RECIPES FOR MEN UNDER 200, 300, 400 & 500 CALORIES

ISBN 978-1-909855-69-4

INTRODUCTION

Personal blending is the fastest way to create super healthy, delicious single serving smoothies, juices, breakfast drinks, protein & nutrition shakes.

This no-fuss approach to a healthier way of living is a great way to increase your fruit intake, compliment your daily workouts, manage your diet or just have fun making great tasting drinks.

Blend & Go devices are hugely popular especially for the health conscious and those with a busy lifestyle. Using the Blend Active couldn't be simpler…just add the ingredients as per our recipes, blend in the sports bottle then replace the blade with the leak proof lid and you're done! It's perfect for quick breakfast drinks on the go, gym nutrition or a meal-time filler if you are on a diet.

All the recipes in this book have been tested using the Breville Blend Active Personal Blender but they can be used for any of the personal blenders on the market. The Breville Blend Active is a great single server blender. The most popular version comes with 2 x 600ml sports bottles with a one-touch blend button. The base unit is small, easy to clean and the blade is even strong enough to crush ice.

Adopting personal blending into your daily routine has enormous health benefits. Balancing your diet with healthy nutritious drinks can help you lose weight as part of a calorie controlled diet, boost your immune system and help fight a number of ailments. Each of the recipes in The Skinny Blend Active & Personal Blender Recipe Book are calorie counted making it easy for you to keep track of your calorific intake and help you achieve your 5-A-Day quota.

Using our recipes and your personal blender on a daily basis together with an overall healthy eating plan will help you feel brighter, rejuvenated, more focused and energetic. We hope you enjoy our recipes!

TIPS

Personal blenders are simple and easy to use. Follow these tips to get the most from your device:

• When using ice in your drink, always immerse the ice first in a little liquid. You can do this in the sports bottle with the liquid ingredients you are using such as a little water or fruit juice.
• When you are adding ingredients don't fill the sports bottle above the 600ml mark (or 300ml if you use are the 300ml bottles).

- If some ingredients become stuck around the blade just detach the bottle from the base unit and give it a good shake to loosen the ingredients then blend again.

- Clean the blender base unit with a damp cloth. The blade, bottle and cap can all be placed in a dishwasher or alternatively wash with warm soapy water. For best results wash parts immediately after using.

- For stubborn ingredients that may have stuck to the blade or the inside of the bottle, half fill the bottle with warm water and a drop or two of detergent, fit the blade and attach to the base unit pulsing for 10 seconds or so.

- Use the freshest produce available. We recommend buying organic produce whenever you can if your budget allows. You can also freeze your fruit to preserve it.

- Wash your fruit and veg before blending to remove any traces of bacteria, pesticides and insects.

- Chop ingredients, especially harder produce, into small pieces to ensure smoother blending.

- Substitute where you need to. If you can't source a particular ingredient, try another instead. Experiment and enjoy!

ALL RECIPES ARE A GUIDE ONLY

All the recipes in this book are a guide only. You may need to alter quantities and cooking times to suit your own appliances.

ABOUT COOKNATION

CookNation is the leading publisher of innovative and practical recipe books for the modern, health conscious cook.

CookNation titles bring together delicious, easy and practical recipes with their unique approach - easy and delicious, no-nonsense recipes - making cooking for diets and healthy eating fast, simple and fun.

With a range of #1 best-selling titles - from the innovative 'Skinny' calorie-counted series, to the 5:2 Diet Recipes collection - CookNation recipe books prove that 'Diet' can still mean 'Delicious'!

Turn to the end of this book to browse all CookNation's recipe books

 **CookNation**

THE *Skinny* BLEND ACTIVE

Under 200 Calories

CINNAMON BERRY JUICE

185 calories per serving

Ingredients

- 1 banana
- 100g/3½oz strawberries
- 50g/2oz raspberries
- 50g/2oz fresh pineapple
- ½ tsp ground cinnamon
- Water

Method

1 Rinse all the ingredients well.

2 Peel the banana and break into small pieces.

3 Add all the fruit & vegetables to the bottle, making sure the ingredients do not go past the 600ml/20oz line on your bottle.

4 Add water, again being careful not to exceed the MAX line.

5 Twist on the blade and blend until smooth.

CHEFS NOTE

Fresh or tinned pineapple will work just as well. Use a little of the juice in place of water if you like.

RASPBERRY ALMOND SMOOTHIE

165 calories per serving

Ingredients

- 1 handful of spinach
- 1 carrot
- 200g/7oz raspberries
- 250ml/1 cup almond milk
- Water

FIBRE RICH!

Method

1 Rinse all the ingredients well.

2 Remove any thick, hard stems from the spinach and roughly chop.

3 Top, tail, peel & chop the carrot.

4 Add the vegetables, fruit & almond milk to the bottle, making sure the ingredients do not go past the 600ml/20oz line on your bottle.

5 Top up with water if needed, again being careful not to exceed the MAX line.

6 Twist on the blade and blend until smooth.

CHEFS NOTE
Strawberries are also good in this lovely smoothie blend.

PAPAYA & BANANA JUICE

195 calories per serving

Ingredients

- 1 banana
- 1 papaya fruit
- 1 kiwi
- Water

VITAMIN C SOURCE

Method

1 Rinse all the ingredients well.

2 Peel the banana and break into small pieces.

3 Peel and chop the kiwi.

4 Scoop out the papaya flesh, discarding the seeds and rind.

5 Add the fruit to the bottle, making sure the ingredients do not go past the 600ml/20oz line on your bottle.

6 Top up with water, again being careful not to exceed the MAX line.

7 Twist on the blade and blend until smooth.

CHEFS NOTE
Native to tropical America, papayas are also known as paw-paws. They are sweet & juicy with a similar taste to peaches.

ICED CHERRY JUICE

170 calories per serving

Ingredients

- 1 handful of spinach
- 1 apple
- 150g/5oz cherries
- Handful of Ice
- Water

TRY WITHOUT SPINACH

Method

1 Rinse all the ingredients well.

2 Remove any thick, hard stems from the spinach and roughly chop.

3 Peel, core and chop the apple.

4 Pit the cherries and remove the stalks.

5 Add the vegetables & fruit to the bottle, making sure the ingredients do not go past the 600ml/20oz line on your bottle.

6 Top up with water and a few ice cubes, again being careful not to exceed the MAX line.

7 Twist on the blade and blend until smooth.

CHEFS NOTE
Frozen cherries are also a good option for this juice and make it even quicker to prepare.

FRUITY SPICED PINEAPPLE JUICE

110 calories per serving

Ingredients

- 1 handful of spinach
- 200g/7oz pineapple chunks
- ½ red chilli
- Water

SPICY!

Method

1 Rinse all the ingredients well.

2 Remove any thick, hard stems from the spinach and roughly chop.

3 De-seed the chilli and finely chop.

4 Add the vegetables, fruit & chopped chilli to the bottle, making sure the ingredients do not go past the 600ml/20oz line on your bottle.

5 Top up with water, again being careful not to exceed the MAX line.

6 Twist on the blade and blend until smooth.

CHEFS NOTE

Use a little cayenne pepper if you don't have fresh chillies to hand.

APPLE GREENS JUICE

185
calories per
serving

Ingredients

- 200g/7oz tenderstem broccoli/ broccolini
- 1 apple
- 1 carrot
- Water

VITAMIN A SOURCE

Method

1 Rinse all the ingredients well.

2 Chop the broccoli.

3 Peel, core & chop the apple.

4 Top, tail, peel and chop the carrot.

5 Add the vegetables & fruit to the bottle, making sure the ingredients do not go past the 600ml/20oz line on your bottle.

6 Top up with water, again being careful not to exceed the MAX line.

7 Twist on the blade and blend until smooth.

CHEFS NOTE
Purple sprouting broccoli stems are a great seasonal ingredient.

ASPARAGUS & APPLE JUICE

155
calories per serving

Ingredients

- 150g/5oz asparagus tips
- 1 apple
- ½ cucumber
- Water

← **GREEN GOODNESS**

Method

1 Rinse all the ingredients well.

2 Chop the asparagus tips.

3 Peel, core & chop the apple.

4 Peel & chop the cucumber.

5 Add the vegetables & fruit to the bottle, making sure the ingredients do not go past the 600ml/20oz line on your bottle.

6 Top up with water, again being careful not to exceed the MAX line.

7 Twist on the blade and blend until smooth.

CHEFS NOTE
This is a really simple juice, add an extra chopped apple if you want a sweeter taste.

PEAR PICK UP JUICE

170 calories per serving

Ingredients

- 1 pear
- 1 apple
- 2 tsp grated fresh ginger root
- 2 tsp lemon juice
- Water

ANTIOXIDANTS

Method

1 Rinse all the ingredients well.

2 Peel, core and chop the pear & apple.

3 Add the fruit, vegetables, ginger & lemon juice to the bottle, making sure the ingredients do not go past the 600ml/20oz line on your bottle.

4 Top up with water, again being careful not to exceed the MAX line.

5 Twist on the blade and blend until smooth.

CHEFS NOTE

Adjust the freshly grated ginger to suit your own taste.

FRUIT VITAMIN C+ JUICE

180 calories per serving

Ingredients

- 1 orange
- 1 banana
- 1 tbsp lemon juice
- Water

USE NAVAL ORANGES

Method

1 Rinse all the ingredients well.

2 Peel and chop the orange, discard the rind.

3 Peel the banana and break into small pieces.

4 Add the fruit, vegetables & lemon juice to the bottle, making sure the ingredients do not go past the 600ml/20oz line on your bottle.

5 Top up with water, again being careful not to exceed the MAX line.

6 Twist on the blade and blend until smooth.

CHEFS NOTE
Orange is the classic Vitamin C provider.

SUPER SALAD JUICE

45 calories per serving

Ingredients

- 1 handful of spinach
- 2 celery stalks
- 1 vine ripened tomato
- ½ cucumber
- ½ tsp cayenne pepper (optional)
- Water

Method

1 Rinse all the ingredients well.

2 Remove any thick, hard stems from the spinach and roughly chop.

3 Chop the celery, discarding any tops.

4 Chop the tomato. Peel & chop the cucumber.

5 Add the chopped salad & cayenne pepper to the bottle, making sure the ingredients do not go past the 600ml/20oz line on your bottle.

6 Top up with water, again being careful not to exceed the MAX line.

7 Twist on the blade and blend until smooth.

CHEFS NOTE

This is a really light juice, great for fresh summer mornings.

CLEANSING APPLE JUICE

110 calories per serving

Ingredients

- 1 apple
- 1 cucumber
- 1 tbsp lime juice
- Water

USE SWEET APPLES

Method

1 Rinse all the ingredients well.

2 Peel, core & chop the apple.

3 Peel & chop the cucumber.

4 Add the chopped fruit, vegetables & lime juice to the bottle, making sure the ingredients do not go past the 600ml/20oz line on your bottle.

5 Top up with water, again being careful not to exceed the MAX line.

6 Twist on the blade and blend until smooth.

CHEFS NOTE
Put some of the cucumber to one side if you can't fit it all in.

COCONUT CHIA JUICE

180 calories per serving

Ingredients

- 1 handful of spinach
- 1 apple
- 2 tsp chia seeds
- 250ml/1 cup coconut water
- Water

LOW CHOLESTEROL

Method

1 Rinse all the ingredients well.

2 Remove any thick, hard stems from the spinach and roughly chop.

3 Peel, core & chop the apple.

4 Add the chopped fruit, vegetables, chia seeds & coconut water to the bottle, making sure the ingredients do not go past the 600ml/20oz line on your bottle.

5 Top up with water if it needs it, again being careful not to exceed the MAX line.

6 Twist on the blade and blend until smooth.

CHEFS NOTE
Chia seeds are a great source of Vitamin B.

DOUBLE PEAR & PAK CHOI JUICE

185 calories per serving

······ *Ingredients* ······

- 1 pak choi/bok choy
- 2 pears
- ½ banana
- Water

LIGHT & FRESH!

······ *Method* ······

1 Rinse all the ingredients well.

2 Shred the pak choi, remove any hard bulb parts.

3 Peel, core & chop the pears.

4 Peel the banana then break into small pieces.

5 Add the chopped fruit & vegetables to the bottle, making sure the ingredients do not go past the 600ml/20oz line on your bottle.

6 Top up with water, again being careful not to exceed the MAX line.

7 Twist on the blade and blend until smooth.

CHEFS NOTE

Pak choi is a great juice alternative to spinach and kale.

APPLE & LEMON JUICE

115 calories per serving

Ingredients

- 2 handfuls of spinach
- 1 apple
- 1 tbsp lemon juice
- Water

ADD 1 TSP HONEY

Method

1 Rinse all the ingredients well.

2 Remove any thick, hard stems from the spinach and roughly chop.

3 Peel, core and chop the apple.

4 Add the fruit, vegetables & lemon juice to the bottle, making sure the ingredients do not go past the 600ml/20oz line on your bottle.

5 Top up with water, again being careful not to exceed the MAX line.

6 Twist on the blade and blend until smooth.

CHEFS NOTE

Give the bottle a good shake mid-way through blending if you find all the ingredients aren't coming together.

GREEN DETOX JUICE

85 calories per serving

Ingredients

- 1 handful of spinach
- 1 handful of kale
- 1 pear
- 1 tbsp lemon juice
- Water

SUPER GREEN JUICE

Method

1 Rinse all the ingredients well.

2 Remove any thick, hard stems from the spinach and kale & roughly chop.

3 Peel, core and chop the pear.

4 Add the fruit, vegetables & lemon juice to the bottle, making sure the ingredients do not go past the 600ml/20oz line on your bottle.

5 Top up with water, again being careful not to exceed the MAX line.

6 Twist on the blade and blend until smooth.

CHEFS NOTE

Add a teaspoon of honey if you struggle with the taste of some of the kale based juices.

MULTI GREEN JUICE

115 calories per serving

Ingredients

- 1 handful of spinach
- 1 handful of pak choi/bok choi
- 1 apple
- Water

USE SWEET APPLES

Method

1 Rinse all the ingredients well.

2 Remove any thick, hard stems from the spinach & pak choi and roughly chop.

3 Peel, core and chop the apple.

4 Add the fruit & vegetables to the bottle, making sure the ingredients do not go past the 600ml/20oz line on your bottle.

5 Top up with water, again being careful not to exceed the MAX line.

6 Twist on the blade and blend until smooth.

CHEFS NOTE

Pak choi is an Asian style cabbage which is now widely available in most stores.

SUPER SALAD JUICE

55
calories per
serving

Ingredients

- 2 celery stalks
- 2 vine ripened tomatoes
- ½ cucumber
- 2 tsp Worcestershire sauce (optional)
- Water

LOW CALORIE

Method

1 Rinse all the ingredients well.

2 Chop the celery, discarding any tops.

3 Chop the tomatoes. Peel & chop the cucumber.

4 Add the chopped salad & Worcestershire sauce to the bottle, making sure the ingredients do not go past the 600ml/20oz line on your bottle.

5 Top up with water, again being careful not to exceed the MAX line.

6 Twist on the blade and blend until smooth.

CHEFS NOTE

This is not a completely smooth juice, but that's not a problem. Just drink the 'bits'!

INDIAN SUMMER JUICE

135
calories per
serving

Ingredients

- 1 handful of spinach
- 1 apple
- 1 carrot
- ½ tsp ground turmeric
- Water

TRY CUMIN

Method

1 Rinse all the ingredients well.

2 Remove any thick, hard stems from the spinach and roughly chop.

3 Peel, core and chop the apple.

4 Top, tail, peel and chop the carrot.

5 Add the vegetables, fruit & turmeric to the bottle, making sure the ingredients do not go past the 600ml/20oz line on your bottle.

6 Top up with water, again being careful not to exceed the MAX line.

7 Twist on the blade and blend until smooth.

CHEFS NOTE
Turmeric adds colour and spice to this unusual juice. Try a pinch of cayenne pepper too.

CRISP LETTUCE & CARROT JUICE

170 calories per serving

Ingredients

- 1 baby gem lettuce
- 1 apple
- 2 carrots
- Water

LIGHT & CRISP!

Method

1 Rinse all the ingredients well.

2 Roughly chop the lettuce and discard the heart.

3 Peel, core and cube the apple.

4 Top, tail, peel and chop the carrots.

5 Add the vegetables & fruit to the bottle, making sure the ingredients do not go past the 600ml/20oz line on your bottle.

6 Top up with water, again being careful not to exceed the MAX line.

7 Twist on the blade and blend until smooth.

CHEFS NOTE
This simple juice is packed with vitamin A.

LEMON & MINT JUICE

125 calories per serving

Ingredients

- 1 baby gem lettuce
- 1 apple
- 3 tbsp lemon juice
- 1 tbsp chopped fresh mint
- 250ml/1 cup coconut water
- Water

Method

1 Rinse all the ingredients well.

2 Roughly chop the lettuce, discard the 'heart'.

3 Peel, core and cube the apple.

4 Add the fruit, salad, coconut water & mint to the bottle, making sure the ingredients do not go past the 600ml/20oz line on your bottle.

5 Top up with water if needed, again being careful not to exceed the MAX line.

6 Twist on the blade and blend until smooth.

CHEFS NOTE
Try using basil as an alternative to mint.

FRUIT GINGER BLAST

180 calories per serving

Ingredients

- 1 handful of spinach
- ½ fresh beetroot
- 1 banana

- 200g/7oz blueberries
- 2 tsp fresh grated ginger root
- Water

Method

1 Rinse all the ingredients well.

2 Peel and dice the beetroot.

3 Peel the banana and break into small pieces.

4 Add all the fruit & vegetables to the bottle, making sure the ingredients do not go past the 600ml/20oz line on your bottle.

5 Add water, again being careful not to exceed the MAX line.

6 Twist on the blade and blend until smooth.

CHEFS NOTE
Try adding a teaspoon of flax seeds for an extra boost.

GREEN BLASTER JUICE

170
calories per serving

Ingredients

- 1 handful of kale
- 1 baby gem lettuce
- 1 apple
- 1 carrot
- Water

TRY GINGER

Method

1 Rinse all the ingredients well.

2 Remove any thick, hard stems from the kale and roughly chop.

3 Roughly chop the lettuce and discard the heart.

4 Peel, core and chop the apple.

5 Top, tail, peel and chop the carrot.

6 Add the vegetables & fruit to the bottle, making sure the ingredients do not go past the 600ml/20oz line on your bottle.

7 Top up with water, again being careful not to exceed the MAX line.

8 Twist on the blade and blend until smooth.

CHEFS NOTE
Spinach and spring greens will work in place of kale.

THE *Skinny*
BLEND ▸*ACTIVE*

Under 300 Calories

VERY BERRY JUICE

220 calories per serving

Ingredients

- 200g/7oz mixed berries
- 1 banana
- 1 tsp honey
- Water

TRY RASPBERRIES

Method

1 Rinse all the ingredients well.

2 Peel the banana and break into small pieces.

3 Add the fruit and honey to the bottle, making sure the ingredients do not go past the 600ml/20oz line on your bottle.

4 Top up with water, again being careful not to exceed the MAX line.

5 Twist on the blade and blend until smooth.

CHEFS NOTE
Frozen mixed berries are a handy ingredient for this simple smoothie.

HONEYED FIG SMOOTHIE

270 calories per serving

Ingredients

- 1 banana
- 3 dried figs
- 250ml/1 cup soya milk
- 2 tsp honey
- Water

DIETARY FIBRE

Method

1 Peel the banana and break into small pieces.

2 Chop the figs.

3 Add the fruit, milk & honey to the bottle, making sure the ingredients do not go past the 600ml/20oz line on your bottle.

4 Top up with water if it needs it, again being careful not to exceed the MAX line.

5 Twist on the blade and blend until smooth.

CHEFS NOTE
Soak the dried figs for half an hour in a little warm water before chopping.

FRESH CHERRY & BANANA SMOOTHIE

260 calories per serving

Ingredients

- 200g/7oz fresh cherries
- 1 banana
- 250ml/1 cup almond milk
- Water

TRY SOYA MILK

Method

1 Rinse all the ingredients well.

2 De-stone, de-stalk and chop the cherries.

3 Peel the banana and break into small pieces.

4 Add the fruit & milk to the bottle, making sure the ingredients do not go past the 600ml/20oz line on your bottle.

5 Top up with water if it needs it, again being careful not to exceed the MAX line.

6 Twist on the blade and blend until smooth.

CHEFS NOTE

Fresh cherries are fabulous when they are in season but frozen cherries will work too if that's all you can get your hands on.

KIWI & SOYA MILK SMOOTHIE

295 calories per serving

Ingredients

- 2 kiwis
- 1 banana
- 250ml/1 cup soya milk
- Water

TRY ALMOND MILK

Method

1 Peel and chop the kiwis.

2 Peel the banana and break into small pieces.

3 Add the fruit & milk to the bottle, making sure the ingredients do not go past the 600ml/20oz line on your bottle.

4 Top up with water if it needs it, again being careful not to exceed the MAX line.

5 Twist on the blade and blend until smooth.

CHEFS NOTE

Use ripe kiwis to make the most of their natural sweetness.

SPINACH & PEAR SMOOTHIE

290 calories per serving

Ingredients

- 1 handful spinach
- 1 banana
- 1 pear
- 1 cup/250ml semi skimmed milk

GOOD & GREEN

Method

1 Remove any thick, hard stems from the spinach and roughly chop.

2 Peel the banana and break into small pieces

3 Peel, core and chop the pear.

4 Add the fruit, vegetables & milk to the bottle, making sure the ingredients do not go past the 600ml/20oz line on your bottle.

5 Twist on the blade and blend until smooth.

CHEFS NOTE
Try using a fresh peach in place of the pear.

PINEAPPLE ICE CRUSH

205 calories per serving

Ingredients

- 1 apple
- 200g/7oz pineapple chunks
- Handful of ice cubes
- Water

REFRESHING!

Method

1 Rinse all the ingredients well.

2 Peel, core and chop the apple.

3 Add the fruit to the bottle, making sure the ingredients do not go past the 600ml/20oz line on your bottle.

4 Top up with the ice and water, again being careful not to exceed the MAX line.

5 Twist on the blade and blend until smooth.

CHEFS NOTE

Pineapple is a great source of manganese and vitamin C.

FRESH HERB JUICE

215 calories per serving

Ingredients

- 1 handful of spinach
- 2 tbsp chopped of fresh mint
- 2 tbsp chopped of fresh basil
- 2 apples
- Water

FRAGRANT!

Method

1 Rinse all the ingredients well.

2 Remove any thick, hard stems from the spinach and roughly chop.

3 Peel, core and chop the apples.

4 Add the fruit, vegetables & herbs to the bottle, making sure the ingredients do not go past the 600ml/20oz line on your bottle.

5 Top up with water, again being careful not to exceed the MAX line.

6 Twist on the blade and blend until smooth.

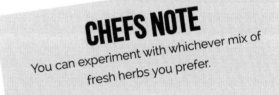

CHEFS NOTE

You can experiment with whichever mix of fresh herbs you prefer.

ALMOND & PINEAPPLE JUICE

260 calories per serving

Ingredients

- 1 handful of spinach
- 1 banana
- 200g/7oz pineapple chunks
- 1 tbsp ground almonds
- Water

USE RIPE BANANA

Method

1 Rinse all the ingredients well.

2 Remove any thick, hard stems from the spinach and roughly chop.

3 Peel the banana and break into small pieces.

4 Add the fruit, vegetables & ground almonds to the bottle, making sure the ingredients do not go past the 600ml/20oz line on your bottle.

5 Top up with water, again being careful not to exceed the MAX line.

6 Twist on the blade and blend until smooth.

CHEFS NOTE

Try using almond milk in place of water as the base for this blend.

PARSLEY & APPLE JUICE

210 calories per serving

Ingredients

- 1 handful of spinach
- 2 apples
- 2 tbsp chopped flat leaf parsley
- 1 tbsp lemon juice
- Water

QUICK & EASY!

Method

1 Rinse all the ingredients well.

2 Remove any thick, hard stems from the spinach and roughly chop.

3 Peel, core and chop the apples.

4 Add the fruit, vegetables, parsley & lemon juice to the bottle, making sure the ingredients do not go past the 600ml/20oz line on your bottle.

5 Top up with water, again being careful not to exceed the MAX line.

6 Twist on the blade and blend until smooth.

CHEFS NOTE
Flat leaf parsley works better than the curly variety for this juice.

PINEAPPLE PEPPER JUICE

260
calories per
serving

Ingredients

- 1 orange pepper
- 1 banana
- 200g/7oz pineapple chunks
- Water

VITAMIN C +

Method

1 Rinse all the ingredients well.

2 De-seed and chop the pepper.

3 Peel the banana and break into small pieces.

4 Add the fruit & vegetables to the bottle, making sure the ingredients do not go past the 600ml/20oz line on your bottle.

5 Top up with water, again being careful not to exceed the MAX line.

6 Twist on the blade and blend until smooth.

CHEFS NOTE
Use whichever peppers you have to hand but avoid green peppers as they tend to be a little bitter in juice blends.

CALYPSO JUICE

250 calories per serving

Ingredients

- 1 handful of spinach
- 1 banana
- 200g/7oz pineapple chunks
- 250ml/1 cup coconut water
- Water

TROPICAL!

Method

1 Rinse all the ingredients well.

2 Remove any thick, hard stems from the spinach and roughly chop.

3 Peel the banana and break into small pieces.

4 Add the fruit, vegetables & coconut water to the bottle, making sure the ingredients do not go past the 600ml/20oz line on your bottle.

5 Top up with water if it needs it, again being careful not to exceed the MAX line.

6 Twist on the blade and blend until smooth.

CHEFS NOTE
Coconut water is a great juice ingredient with low levels of fat, carbohydrates, and calories.

SKINNY GREEN JUICE

230
calories per
serving

Ingredients

- 2 apples
- 1 courgette/zucchini
- ½ cucumber
- Water

USE SWEET APPLES

Method

1 Rinse all the ingredients well.

2 Peel, core and chop the apples.

3 Peel the courgette and cucumber. Top & tail them both before chopping.

4 Add the vegetables & fruit to the bottle, making sure the ingredients do not go past the 600ml/20oz line on your bottle.

5 Top up with water, again being careful not to exceed the MAX line.

6 Twist on the blade and blend until smooth.

CHEFS NOTE
This is a subtly tasting super-cleansing juice bursting with fresh goodness.

ORANGE BLAST

210
calories per
serving

Ingredients

- 1 orange
- 1 apple
- 1 carrot
- 1 tbsp fresh chopped basil
- Water

ADD ORANGE ZEST

Method

1 Rinse all the ingredients well.

2 Peel the orange and chop, discard the seeds.

3 Peel, core and chop the apple.

4 Top, tail, peel & chop the carrot.

5 Add the vegetables, fruit & basil to the bottle, making sure the ingredients do not go past the 600ml/20oz line on your bottle.

6 Top up with water, again being careful not to exceed the MAX line.

7 Twist on the blade and blend until smooth.

CHEFS NOTE
Adjust the quantity of fresh basil to suit your own taste.

REFRESHING LIME & CRANBERRY JUICE

295 calories per serving

······ *Ingredients* ······

- 2 apples
- 2 tbsp lime juice
- 200g/7oz fresh cranberries
- Water

TRY FROZEN CRANBERRIES

······ *Method* ······

1 Rinse all the ingredients well.

2 Peel, core and chop the apples.

3 Add the fruit & lime juice to the bottle, making sure the ingredients do not go past the 600ml/20oz line on your bottle.

4 Top up with water, again being careful not to exceed the MAX line.

5 Twist on the blade and blend until smooth.

CHEFS NOTE
Adjust the quantity of lime juice to suit your own taste.

GOOD GRAPEFRUIT JUICE

220 calories per serving

Ingredients

- 1 pink grapefruit
- 200g/7oz pineapple chunks
- 2 tsp honey
- Water

SWEET!

Method

1 Rinse all the ingredients well.

2 Peel and chop the grapefruit, discarding any seeds.

3 Add the fruit & honey to the bottle, making sure the ingredients do not go past the 600ml/20oz line on your bottle.

4 Top up with water, again being careful not to exceed the MAX line.

5 Twist on the blade and blend until smooth.

CHEFS NOTE
Good & Green: this is a simple and tasty morning juice.

FRUITY GRAPE JUICE

220
calories per
serving

Ingredients

- 1 handful of spinach
- 1 pear
- 200g/7oz green seedless grapes
- Water

VITAMIN K +

Method

1 Rinse all the ingredients well.

2 Remove any thick, hard stems from the spinach and roughly chop.

3 Peel, core and chop the pear.

4 Remove the stalks from the grapes.

5 Add the vegetables & fruit to the bottle, making sure the ingredients do not go past the 600ml/20oz line on your bottle.

6 Top up with water, again being careful not to exceed the MAX line.

7 Twist on the blade and blend until smooth.

CHEFS NOTE
Red grapes are just as good in this juice.

FAST FRUIT SALAD

230
calories per serving

Ingredients

- 1 handful of spinach or spring greens
- 1 baby gem lettuce
- 1 banana
- 1 apple
- Water

LIGHT & FRESH!

Method

1 Rinse all the ingredients well.

2 Remove any thick, hard stems from the spinach and roughly chop.

3 Chop the lettuce, discard the heart.

4 Peel the banana and break into small pieces.

5 Peel, core and chop the apple.

6 Add the vegetables & fruit to the bottle, making sure the ingredients do not go past the 600ml/20oz line on your bottle.

7 Top up with water, again being careful not to exceed the MAX line.

8 Twist on the blade and blend until smooth.

CHEFS NOTE
Fast and fresh this is a lovely light juice.

SIMPLE STRAWBERRY SMOOTHIE

299 calories per serving

······· *Ingredients* ·······

- 1 banana
- 200g/7oz strawberries
- 250ml/1 cup semi skimmed milk
- Water

 **CREAMY!**

······· *Method* ·······

1 Rinse all the ingredients well.

2 Peel the banana and break into small pieces.

3 Cut the green tops of the strawberries and chop.

4 Add the fruit & milk to the bottle, making sure the ingredients do not go past the 600ml/20oz line on your bottle.

5 Top up with water if needed, again being careful not to exceed the MAX line.

6 Twist on the blade and blend until smooth.

CHEFS NOTE
Add more banana for extra creaminess.

MANGO BOOST JUICE

280 calories per serving

Ingredients

- 1 apple
- 200g/7oz mango
- 1 kiwi
- Water

USE RIPE MANGO

Method

1 Rinse all the ingredients well.

2 Peel, core and chop the apple.

3 De-stone the mango and chop the flesh, discarding the rind.

4 Peel & chop the kiwi.

5 Add the fruit to the bottle, making sure the ingredients do not go past the 600ml/20oz line on your bottle.

6 Top up with water, again being careful not to exceed the MAX line.

7 Twist on the blade and blend until smooth.

CHEFS NOTE
Kiwi is an excellent source of vitamin 'C'.

HONEY & SWEET POTATO SMOOTHIE

285 calories per serving

Ingredients

- 1 apple
- 200g/7oz sweet potato
- 250ml/1 cup almond milk
- 2 tsp runny honey
- Water

TRY SOYA MILK

Method

1 Rinse all the ingredients well.

2 Peel, core and chop the apple.

3 Peel and chop the sweet potato.

4 Add the vegetables, fruit & milk to the bottle, making sure the ingredients do not go past the 600ml/20oz line on your bottle.

5 Top up with water if it needs it, again being careful not to exceed the MAX line.

6 Twist on the blade and blend until smooth.

CHEFS NOTE

Adjust the honey and almond milk to suit your own taste.

PINEAPPLE & GINGER JUICE

210 calories per serving

Ingredients

- 1 tbsp lemon juice
- 1 banana
- 200g/7oz pineapple chunks
- 1 tsp grated fresh ginger root
- Water

SWEET & SPICY!

Method

1 Rinse all the ingredients well.

2 Peel the banana and break into small pieces.

3 Add the fruit and lemon juice to the bottle, making sure the ingredients do not go past the 600ml/20oz line on your bottle.

4 Top up with water, again being careful not to exceed the MAX line.

5 Twist on the blade and blend until smooth.

CHEFS NOTE
Ginger has been used for centuries as a natural treatment for coughs and colds.

ICY FRUIT CHARD

240
calories per serving

Ingredients

- 1 small handful Swiss chard leaves
- 1 banana
- 200g/7oz fresh pineapple chunks
- Water
- Handful of ice

NATURAL SODIUM

Method

1 Rinse all the ingredients well.

2 Roughly chop the chard leaves..

3 Peel the banana and break into small pieces.

4 Chop the pineapple and add all the fruit & salad to the bottle, making sure the ingredients do not go past the 600ml/20oz line on your bottle.

5 Top up with water & ice, again being careful not to exceed the MAX line.

6 Twist on the blade and blend until smooth.

CHEFS NOTE
Try using spinach if you find chard a little bitter.

CITRUS ALMOND MILK

250 calories per serving

Ingredients

- 1 orange
- 200g/7oz mixed berries
- 250ml/1 cup almond milk
- 2 tsp honey
- 25g/1oz fresh walnuts
- Water

Method

1 Rinse all the ingredients well.

2 Peel the orange and roughly chop (discard any seeds).

3 Add the fruit, milk, honey & walnuts to the bottle, making sure the ingredients do not go past the 600ml/20oz line on your bottle.

4 Top up with water if needed, again being careful not to exceed the MAX line.

5 Twist on the blade and blend until smooth.

CHEFS NOTE
Chop the walnuts before blending for a smooth finish.

CREAMY COCONUT JUICE

275 calories per serving

Ingredients

- 1 apple
- 1 banana
- 250ml/1 cup coconut water
- ½ tsp ground cinnamon
- Water

TRY GROUND NUTMEG

Method

1 Rinse all the ingredients well.

2 Peel, core and dice the apple.

3 Peel the banana and break into small pieces.

4 Add the fruit & coconut water to the bottle, making sure the ingredients do not go past the 600ml/20oz line on your bottle.

5 Top up with water if needed, again being careful not to exceed the MAX line.

6 Twist on the blade and blend until smooth.

CHEFS NOTE
Try adding tablespoon of coconut cream if you want a richer blend.

SERVES 1

PINEAPPLE & COCONUT WATER

255 calories per serving

Ingredients

- 1 banana
- 200g/7oz fresh pineapple
- 250ml/1 cup coconut water
- Water

TRY AN EXTRA BANANA

Method

1 Rinse all the ingredients well.

2 Peel the banana and break into small pieces.

3 Add the fruit & coconut water to the bottle, making sure the ingredients do not go past the 600ml/20oz line on your bottle.

4 Top up with water if needed, again being careful not to exceed the MAX line.

5 Twist on the blade and blend until smooth.

CHEFS NOTE
Try adding two tablespoons of acai berries to this blend for extra goodness.

BANANA OATS

235
calories per
serving

Ingredients

- 1 banana
- 1 apple
- 2 tbsp rolled oats
- Water

ADD TSP HONEY

Method

1 Rinse all the ingredients well.

2 Peel the banana and break into small pieces.

3 Peel, core and cube the apple.

4 Add the fruit, & oats to the bottle, making sure the ingredients do not go past the 600ml/20oz line on your bottle.

5 Top up with water, again being careful not to exceed the MAX line.

6 Twist on the blade and blend until smooth.

CHEFS NOTE
This is a lovely cleansing blend, great at breakfast time.

MANGO & KIWI JUICE

255 calories per serving

Ingredients

- 1 kiwi fruit
- 150g/5oz fresh mango
- 1 banana
- Water

SKIN CLEANSER

Method

1 Rinse all the ingredients well.

2 Peel & dice the kiwi.

3 De-stone, peel and chop the mango.

4 Peel the banana and break into small pieces.

5 Add the fruit to the bottle, making sure the ingredients do not go past the 600ml/20oz line on your bottle.

6 Top up with water, again being careful not to exceed the MAX line.

7 Twist on the blade and blend until smooth.

CHEFS NOTE
Try making this blend using soya milk instead of water as the base.

NUTTY BANANA SMOOTHIE

275
calories per
serving

Ingredients

- 1 banana
- 25g/1oz cashew nuts
- 2 tsp maple syrup
- Water

TRY GROUND ALMONDS

Method

1 Rinse all the ingredients well.

2 Peel the banana and break into small pieces.

3 Chop the cashews nuts.

4 Add the banana, nuts & syrup to the bottle, making sure the ingredients do not go past the 600ml/20oz line on your bottle.

5 Top up with water, again being careful not to exceed the MAX line.

6 Twist on the blade and blend until smooth.

CHEFS NOTE
For extra nuttiness try making this blend using almond milk instead of water as the base.

TRIPLE GREEN CLEANSER

260 calories per serving

Ingredients

- 1 handful of spinach
- 1 handful of kale
- 50g/2oz green beans

- 1 banana
- 1 apple
- Water

Method

1 Rinse all the ingredients well.

2 Remove any thick, hard stems from the spinach & kale and roughly chop.

3 Top & tail the green beans and roughly chop.

4 Peel the banana and break into small pieces.

5 Peel, core and cube the apple.

6 Add the fruit & vegetables to the bottle, making sure the ingredients do not go past the 600ml/20oz line on your bottle.

7 Top up with water, again being careful not to exceed the MAX line.

8 Twist on the blade and blend until smooth.

CHEFS NOTE

This is a triple blast of green goodness. Adjust the quantities to suit your own taste.

THE *Skinny*
BLEND ▸ *ACTIVE*
Under 400 Calories

SUPER SMOOTH STRAWBERRIES

375 calories per serving

Ingredients

- 200g/7oz strawberries
- ½ ripe avocado
- 250ml/1 cup almond milk
- Water

 UNSATURATED FATS

Method

1 Rinse all the ingredients well.

2 Remove the stalks and chop the strawberries.

3 De-stone the avocado and scoop out the flesh, remove the rind.

4 Add the fruit, avocado & almond milk to the bottle, making sure the ingredients do not go past the 600ml/20oz line on your bottle.

5 Top up with water if needed, again being careful not to exceed the MAX line.

6 Twist on the blade and blend until smooth.

CHEFS NOTE
Raspberries are also good in this smoothie.

NUTTY BLUEBERRY SMOOTHIE

310 calories per serving

Ingredients

- 200g/7oz blueberries
- 1 banana
- 1 tbsp ground almonds
- 250ml/1 cup almond milk
- Water

ANTIOXIDANTS

Method

1 Rinse all the ingredients well.

2 Peel the banana and break into small pieces.

3 Add the fruit, milk & ground almonds to the bottle, making sure the ingredients do not go past the 600ml/20oz line on your bottle.

4 Top up with water if it needs it, again being careful not to exceed the MAX line.

5 Twist on the blade and blend until smooth.

CHEFS NOTE
In place of ground almonds try freshly chopped walnuts.

PROTEIN POWER SMOOTHIE

SERVES 1

360 calories per serving

Ingredients

- 1 banana
- 1 scoop protein powder
- 1 tbsp low fat peanut butter
- 250ml/1 cup almond milk
- Water

USE SMOOTH PEANUT BUTTER

Method

1 Peel the banana and break into small pieces.

2 Add all the ingredients to the bottle, making sure the contents do not go past the 600ml/20oz line on your bottle.

3 Twist on the blade and blend until smooth.

CHEFS NOTE

Most protein powder comes with a measuring scoop. If not just use one level tablespoon of powder.

66

NUTTY CHOCOLATE PROTEIN SMOOTHIE

375 calories per serving

Ingredients

- 1 banana
- 1 scoop protein powder
- 1 tbsp hazelnut chocolate spread
- 250ml/1 cup semi-skimmed milk

PROTEIN POWER!

Method

1 Peel the banana and break into small pieces.

2 Add all the ingredients to the bottle, making sure the contents do not go past the 600ml/20oz line on your bottle.

3 Twist on the blade and blend until smooth.

CHEFS NOTE
Nutella is a great hazelnut chocolate spread but any variety will work fine.

CINNAMON PEACH SMOOTHIE

390 calories per serving

Ingredients

- 1 peach
- 1 apple
- 1 banana

- 250ml/1 cup semi skimmed milk
- Pinch of ground cinnamon
- Water

Method

1 Rinse all the ingredients well.

2 Peel, de-stone and chop the peach

3 Peel, core & chop the apple.

4 Peel the banana and break into small pieces.

5 Add the fruit, milk & cinnamon to the bottle, making sure the ingredients do not go past the 600ml/20oz line on your bottle.

6 Top up with water if it needs it, again being careful not to exceed the MAX line.

7 Twist on the blade and blend until smooth.

CHEFS NOTE
Unsweetened tinned peaches will work just fine in place of fresh peaches.

DOUBLE ALMOND & MANGO SMOOTHIE

355 calories per serving

Ingredients

- 1 mango
- 1 banana
- 250ml/1 cup almond milk
- 1 tbsp ground almonds
- Water

HIGH ENERGY!

Method

1 Peel, de-stone and chop the mango.

2 Peel the banana and break into small pieces.

3 Add the fruit, milk & ground almonds to the bottle, making sure the ingredients do not go past the 600ml/20oz line on your bottle.

4 Top up with water if it needs it, again being careful not to exceed the MAX line.

5 Twist on the blade and blend until smooth.

CHEFS NOTE

You could easily use fresh chopped almonds in place of ground almonds.

BANANA NUT SMOOTHIE

330
calories per serving

Ingredients

- 2 bananas
- 1 tbsp low fat smooth peanut butter
- 1 cup/250ml almond milk

QUICK & EASY!

Method

1 Peel the banana and break into small pieces.

2 Add the bananas, peanut butter & almond milk to the bottle, making sure the ingredients do not go past the 600ml/20oz line on your bottle.

3 Twist on the blade and blend until smooth.

CHEFS NOTE
Use smooth peanut butter rather than the crunchy variety.

STRAWBERRY & PEANUT SMOOTHIE

385 calories per serving

Ingredients

- 200g/7oz strawberries
- 1 banana
- 1 tbsp smooth peanut butter
- 1 cup/250ml semi skimmed milk

SWEET & NUTTY!

Method

1 Remove the green tops and chop the strawberries.

2 Peel the banana and break into small pieces

3 Add the strawberries, banana, peanut butter & milk to the bottle, making sure the ingredients do not go past the 600ml/20oz line on your bottle.

4 Twist on the blade and blend until smooth.

CHEFS NOTE
Soya milk or almond milk will also work well in this smoothie.

AVOCADO & APPLE BLEND

280 calories per serving

Ingredients

- ½ ripe avocado
- 1 apple
- 2 mint leaves
- 1 tsp lime juice
- Water

GOOD FATS

Method

1 Rinse all the ingredients well.

2 De-stone the avocado and scoop out the flesh, discard the rind.

3 Peel, core and chop the apple.

4 Add the fruit, mint & lime jiuce to the bottle, making sure the ingredients do not go past the 600ml/20oz line on your bottle.

5 Top up with water, again being careful not to exceed the MAX line.

6 Twist on the blade and blend until smooth.

CHEFS NOTE

Creamy and light this blend is also good with a touch of spice. Try adding some freshly ground black pepper.

CREAMY GREEN SMOOTHIE

370
calories per serving

Ingredients

- 1 handful of spinach
- ½ ripe avocado
- 1 apple
- 250ml/1 cup soya milk
- Water

VITAMINS A, E & C

Method

1 Rinse all the ingredients well.

2 Remove any thick, hard stems from the spinach and roughly chop.

3 De-stone the avocado and scoop out the flesh, discard the rind.

4 Peel, core and chop the apple.

5 Add the fruit, vegetables & soya milk to the bottle, making sure the ingredients do not go past the 600ml/20oz line on your bottle.

6 Top up with water if needed, again being careful not to exceed the MAX line.

7 Twist on the blade and blend until smooth.

CHEFS NOTE
Try substituting the spinach for kale if you want some 'hardcore' greens.

BANANA & CHIA SEED SMOOTHIE

315 calories per serving

Ingredients

- 2 bananas
- 1 tsp chia seeds
- 250ml/1 cup almond milk
- Water

OMEGA 3 +

Method

1 Rinse all the ingredients well.

2 Peel the bananas and break into small pieces.

3 Add the bananas, chia seeds & almond milk to the bottle, making sure the ingredients do not go past the 600ml/20oz line on your bottle.

4 Top up with water if it needs it, again being careful not to exceed the MAX line.

5 Twist on the blade and blend until smooth.

CHEFS NOTE
Chia seeds are now widely available, they are packed with nutrients.

BREAKFAST OAT SMOOTHIE

395
calories per serving

Ingredients

- 2 bananas
- 1 tbsp rolled oats
- 1 tbsp honey
- 250ml/1 cup soya milk
- Water

ENERGY GIVING!

Method

1 Rinse all the ingredients well.

2 Peel the bananas and break into small pieces.

3 Add the bananas, oats, honey & soya milk to the bottle, making sure the ingredients do not go past the 600ml/20oz line on your bottle.

4 Top up with water if it needs it, again being careful not to exceed the MAX line.

5 Twist on the blade and blend until smooth.

CHEFS NOTE
You can add some chopped apple or pear to this smoothie too if you like.

CASHEW PEACH SMOOTHIE

370 calories per serving

Ingredients

- 1 banana
- 2 peaches
- 50g/2oz cashew nuts
- 250ml/1 cup almond milk
- Water

MILD & SWEET!

Method

1 Rinse all the ingredients well.

2 Peel the banana and break into small pieces.

3 Peel, de-stone and chop the peaches.

4 Chop the cashew nuts.

5 Add the fruit, nuts & almond milk to the bottle, making sure the ingredients do not go past the 600ml/20oz line on your bottle.

6 Top up with water if it needs it, again being careful not to exceed the MAX line.

7 Twist on the blade and blend until smooth.

CHEFS NOTE

Tinned peaches will work just as well if you don't have time to peel fresh peaches.

GOJI BERRY SMOOTHIE

340
calories per serving

Ingredients

- 1 banana
- 200g/7oz strawberries
- 1 tbsp goji berries
- 250ml/1 cup almond milk
- Water

GOJI GOODNESS!

Method

1 Rinse all the ingredients well.

2 Peel the banana and break into small pieces.

3 Remove the green tops from the strawberries and chop.

4 Add the fruit & almond milk to the bottle, making sure the ingredients do not go past the 600ml/20oz line on your bottle.

5 Top up with water if needed, again being careful not to exceed the MAX line.

6 Twist on the blade and blend until smooth.

CHEFS NOTE

Recent studies have indicated that goji berries may help protect against the influenza virus.

BLUEBERRY & AVOCADO JUICE

375
calories per serving

Ingredients

- ½ ripe avocado
- 1 banana
- 200g/7oz blueberries
- 2 tsp honey
- Water

SWEET & FRUITY!

Method

1 Rinse all the ingredients well.

2 De-stone the avocado and scoop out the flesh, discard the rind.

3 Peel the banana and break into small pieces.

4 Add the fruit, avocado & honey to the bottle, making sure the ingredients do not go past the 600ml/20oz line on your bottle.

5 Top up with water, again being careful not to exceed the MAX line.

6 Twist on the blade and blend until smooth.

CHEFS NOTE
You can use any type of sweet berry you prefer.

PINEAPPLE PROTEIN

335
calories per
serving

Ingredients

- 200g/7oz fresh pineapple chunks
- 250ml/1 cup semi skimmed milk
- 1 scoop protein powder
- Water

GREAT GYM BUDDY

Method

1 Rinse all the ingredients well.

2 Add the fruit, milk & protein powder to the bottle, making sure the ingredients do not go past the 600ml/20oz line on your bottle.

3 Top up with water if needed, again being careful not to exceed the MAX line.

4 Twist on the blade and blend until smooth.

CHEFS NOTE

If you don't have protein powder use a handful of cashew nuts instead.

CREAMY AVOCADO SMOOTHIE

320 calories per serving

Ingredients

- ½ ripe avocado
- 1 apple
- 250ml/1 cup almond milk
- Handful of ice

MID MORNING BOOSTER

Method

1 Rinse all the ingredients well.

2 De-stone the avocado and scoop out the flesh, discard the rind.

3 Peel, core and cube the apple.

4 Add the fruit, avocado & almond milk to the bottle, making sure the ingredients do not go past the 600ml/20oz line on your bottle.

5 Add some ice, again being careful not to exceed the MAX line.

6 Twist on the blade and blend until smooth.

CHEFS NOTE
Bursting with 'good' fats this smoothie will get you going in the morning.

APPLE SOYA MILK SMOOTHIE

315 calories per serving

Ingredients

- 1 banana
- 1 apple
- 250ml/1 cup soya milk
- Handful of ice

ADD CHIA SEEDS

Method

1 Rinse all the ingredients well.

2 Peel the banana and break into small pieces.

3 Peel, core and cube the apple.

4 Add the fruit & soya milk to the bottle, making sure the ingredients do not go past the 600ml/20oz line on your bottle.

5 Add some ice, again being careful not to exceed the MAX line.

6 Twist on the blade and blend until smooth.

CHEFS NOTE

Almond milk works well in this smoothie too.

PEAR & ALMOND SMOOTHIE

330
calories per serving

Ingredients

- 2 pears
- 1 banana
- 50g/2oz chopped almonds
- Water

MINERAL RICH!

Method

1 Rinse all the ingredients well.

2 Peel, core and cube the pears.

3 Peel the banana and break into small pieces.

4 Add the fruit & nuts to the bottle, making sure the ingredients do not go past the 600ml/20oz line on your bottle.

5 Top up with water, again being careful not to exceed the MAX line.

6 Twist on the blade and blend until smooth.

CHEFS NOTE
Try topping up with semi skimmed or almond milk rather than water for a thicker blend.

CONVERSION CHART: DRY INGREDIENTS

Metric	Imperial
7g	¼ oz
15g	½ oz
20g	¾ oz
25g	1 oz
40g	1½oz
50g	2oz
60g	2½oz
75g	3oz
100g	3½oz
125g	4oz
140g	4½oz
150g	5oz
165g	5½oz
175g	6oz
200g	7oz
225g	8oz
250g	9oz
275g	10oz
300g	11oz
350g	12oz
375g	13oz
400g	14oz

Metric	Imperial
425g	15oz
450g	1lb
500g	1lb 2oz
550g	1¼lb
600g	1lb 5oz
650g	1lb 7oz
675g	1½lb
700g	1lb 9oz
750g	1lb 11oz
800g	1¾lb
900g	2lb
1kg	2¼lb
1.1kg	2½lb
1.25kg	2¾lb
1.35kg	3lb
1.5kg	3lb 6oz
1.8kg	4lb
2kg	4½lb
2.25kg	5lb
2.5kg	5½lb
2.75kg	6lb

CONVERSION CHART: LIQUID MEASURES

Metric	Imperial	US
25ml	1fl oz	
60ml	2fl oz	¼ cup
75ml	2½ fl oz	
100ml	3½fl oz	
120ml	4fl oz	½ cup
150ml	5fl oz	
175ml	6fl oz	
200ml	7fl oz	
250ml	8½ fl oz	1 cup
300ml	10½ fl oz	
360ml	12½ fl oz	
400ml	14fl oz	
450ml	15½ fl oz	
600ml	1 pint	
750ml	1¼ pint	3 cups
1 litre	1½ pints	4 cups

Other COOKNATION TITLES

If you enjoyed 'The Skinny Blend Active & Personal Blender Recipe Book' we'd really appreciate your feedback. Reviews help others decide if this is the right book for them so a moment of your time would be appreciated.

Thank you.

You may also be interested in other '**Skinny**' titles in the CookNation series. You can find all the following great titles by searching under '**CookNation**'.

THE SKINNY SLOW COOKER RECIPE BOOK

Delicious Recipes Under 300, 400 And 500 Calories.

Paperback / eBook

THE SKINNY INDIAN TAKEAWAY RECIPE BOOK

Authentic British Indian Restaurant Dishes Under 300, 400 And 500 Calories. The Secret To Low Calorie Indian Takeaway Food At Home.

Paperback / eBook

THE HEALTHY KIDS SMOOTHIE BOOK

40 Delicious Goodness In A Glass Recipes for Happy Kids.

eBook

THE SKINNY 5:2 FAST DIET FAMILY FAVOURITES RECIPE BOOK

Eat With All The Family On Your Diet Fasting Days.

Paperback / eBook

THE SKINNY SLOW COOKER VEGETARIAN RECIPE BOOK

40 Delicious Recipes Under 200, 300 And 400 Calories.

Paperback / eBook

THE PALEO DIET FOR BEGINNERS SLOW COOKER RECIPE BOOK

Gluten Free, Everyday Essential Slow Cooker Paleo Recipes For Beginners.

eBook

THE SKINNY 5:2 SLOW COOKER RECIPE BOOK

Skinny Slow Cooker Recipe And Menu Ideas Under 100, 200, 300 & 400 Calories For Your 5:2 Diet.

Paperback / eBook

THE SKINNY 5:2 BIKINI DIET RECIPE BOOK

Recipes & Meal Planners Under 100, 200 & 300 Calories. Get Ready For Summer & Lose Weight...FAST!

Paperback / eBook

THE SKINNY 5:2 FAST DIET MEALS FOR ONE

Single Serving Fast Day Recipes & Snacks Under 100, 200 & 300 Calories.

Paperback / eBook

THE SKINNY HALOGEN OVEN FAMILY FAVOURITES RECIPE BOOK

Healthy, Low Calorie Family Meal-Time Halogen Oven Recipes Under 300, 400 and 500 Calories.

Paperback / eBook

THE SKINNY 5:2 FAST DIET VEGETARIAN MEALS FOR ONE

Single Serving Fast Day Recipes & Snacks Under 100, 200 & 300 Calories.

Paperback / eBook

THE PALEO DIET FOR BEGINNERS MEALS FOR ONE

The Ultimate Paleo Single Serving Cookbook.

Paperback / eBook

THE SKINNY SOUP MAKER RECIPE BOOK

Delicious Low Calorie, Healthy and Simple Soup Recipes Under 100, 200 and 300 Calories. Perfect For Any Diet and Weight Loss Plan.

Paperback / eBook

THE PALEO DIET FOR BEGINNERS HOLIDAYS

Thanksgiving, Christmas & New Year Paleo Friendly Recipes.
eBook

SKINNY HALOGEN OVEN COOKING FOR ONE

Single Serving, Healthy, Low Calorie Halogen Oven RecipesUnder 200, 300 and 400 Calories.

Paperback / eBook

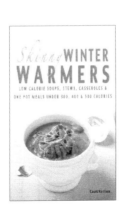

SKINNY WINTER WARMERS RECIPE BOOK

Soups, Stews, Casseroles & One Pot Meals Under 300, 400 & 500 Calories.

Paperback / eBook

THE SKINNY 5:2 DIET RECIPE BOOK COLLECTION

All The 5:2 Fast Diet Recipes You'll Ever Need. All Under 100, 200, 300, 400 And 500 Calories.

eBook

THE SKINNY SLOW COOKER CURRY RECIPE BOOK

Low Calorie Curries From Around The World.

Paperback / eBook

THE SKINNY BREAD MACHINE RECIPE BOOK

70 Simple, Lower Calorie, Healthy Breads...Baked To Perfection In Your Bread Maker.

Paperback / eBook

MORE SKINNY SLOW COOKER RECIPES

75 More Delicious Recipes Under 300, 400 & 500 Calories.

Paperback / eBook

THE SKINNY 5:2 DIET CHICKEN DISHES RECIPE BOOK

Delicious Low Calorie Chicken Dishes Under 300, 400 & 500 Calories.

Paperback / eBook

THE SKINNY 5:2 CURRY RECIPE BOOK

Spice Up Your Fast Days With Simple Low Calorie Curries, Snacks, Soups, Salads & Sides Under 200, 300 & 400 Calories.

Paperback / eBook

THE SKINNY JUICE DIET RECIPE BOOK

5lbs, 5 Days. The Ultimate Kick- Start Diet and Detox Plan to Lose Weight & Feel Great!

Paperback / eBook

THE SKINNY SLOW COOKER SOUP RECIPE BOOK

Simple, Healthy & Delicious Low Calorie Soup Recipes For Your Slow Cooker. All Under 100, 200 & 300 Calories.

Paperback / eBook

THE SKINNY SLOW COOKER SUMMER RECIPE BOOK

Fresh & Seasonal Summer Recipes For Your Slow Cooker. All Under 300, 400 And 500 Calories.

Paperback / eBook

THE SKINNY HOT AIR FRYER COOKBOOK

Delicious & Simple Meals For Your Hot Air Fryer: Discover The Healthier Way To Fry.

Paperback / eBook

THE SKINNY ACTIFRY COOKBOOK

Guilt-free and Delicious ActiFry Recipe Ideas: Discover The Healthier Way to Fry!

Paperback / eBook

THE SKINNY ICE CREAM MAKER

Delicious Lower Fat, Lower Calorie Ice Cream, Frozen Yogurt & Sorbet Recipes For Your Ice Cream Maker.

Paperback / eBook

THE SKINNY 15 MINUTE MEALS RECIPE BOOK

Delicious, Nutritious & Super-Fast Meals in 15 Minutes Or Less. All Under 300, 400 & 500 Calories.

Paperback / eBook

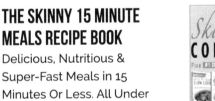

THE SKINNY SLOW COOKER COLLECTION

5 Fantastic Books of Delicious, Diet-friendly Skinny Slow Cooker Recipes: ALL Under 200, 300, 400 & 500 Calories!
eBook

THE SKINNY MEDITERRANEAN RECIPE BOOK

Simple, Healthy & Delicious Low Calorie Mediterranean Diet Dishes. All Under 200, 300 & 400 Calories.

Paperback / eBook

THE SKINNY LOW CALORIE RECIPE BOOK

Great Tasting, Simple & Healthy Meals Under 300, 400 & 500 Calories. Perfect For Any Calorie Controlled Diet.

Paperback / eBook

THE SKINNY TAKEAWAY RECIPE BOOK

Healthier Versions Of Your Fast Food Favourites: All Under 300, 400 & 500 Calories.

Paperback / eBook

THE SKINNY NUTRIBULLET RECIPE BOOK

80+ Delicious & Nutritious Healthy Smoothie Recipes. Burn Fat, Lose Weight and Feel Great!

Paperback / eBook

THE SKINNY NUTRIBULLET SOUP RECIPE BOOK

Delicious, Quick & Easy, Single Serving Soups & Pasta Sauces For Your Nutribullet. All Under 100, 200, 300 & 400 Calories!

Paperback / eBook

THE SKINNY PRESSURE COOKER COOKBOOK

USA ONLY
Low Calorie, Healthy & Delicious Meals, Sides & Desserts. All Under 300, 400 & 500 Calories.

Paperback / eBook

THE SKINNY ONE-POT RECIPE BOOK

Simple & Delicious, One-Pot Meals. All Under 300, 400 & 500 Calories

Paperback / eBook

THE SKINNY NUTRIBULLET MEALS IN MINUTES RECIPE BOOK

Quick & Easy, Single Serving Suppers, Snacks, Sauces, Salad Dressings & More Using Your Nutribullet. All Under 300, 400 & 500 Calories

Paperback / eBook

THE SKINNY STEAMER RECIPE BOOK

Healthy, Low Calorie, Low Fat Steam Cooking Recipes Under 300, 400 & 500 Calories.

Paperback / eBook

MANFOOD: 5:2 FAST DIET MEALS FOR MEN

Simple & Delicious, Fuss Free, Fast Day Recipes For Men Under 200, 300, 400 & 500 Calories.

Paperback / eBook

THE SKINNY SPIRALIZER RECIPE BOOK

Delicious Spiralizer Inspired Low Calorie Recipes For One. All Under 200, 300, 400 & 500 Calories

Paperback / eBook

THE SKINNY SLOW COOKER STUDENT RECIPE BOOK

Delicious, Simple, Low Calorie, Low Budget, Slow Cooker Meals For Hungry Students. All Under 300, 400 & 500 Calories

Paperback / eBook

MANFOOD: GYM DIARY:

The Only Pocket Workout Journal You'll Ever Need

Paperback / eBook

THE SKINNY NUTRIBULLET 7 DAY CLEANSE

Calorie Counted Cleanse & Detox Plan: Smoothies, Soups & Meals to Lose Weight & Feel Great Fast. Real Food. Real Results

Paperback / eBook

THE SKINNY 30 MINUTE MEALS RECIPE BOOK

Great Food, Easy Recipes, Prepared & Cooked In 30 Minutes Or Less. All Under 300, 400 & 500 Calories

Paperback / eBook

POSH TOASTIES

Simple & Delicious Gourmet Recipes For Your Toastie Machine, Sandwich Grill Or Panini Press

Paperback / eBook

THE SKINNY EXPRESS CURRY RECIPE BOOK

Quick & Easy Authentic Low Fat Indian Dishes Under 300, 400 & 500 Calories

Paperback / eBook

THE SKINNY SPIRALIZER SOUP RECIPE BOOK

Delicious Spiralizer Inspired Soup Recipes All Under 100, 200, 300 & 400 Calories

Paperback / eBook

THE SKINNY NUTRIBULLET
COCKTAIL RECIPE BOOK

Have a Blast with your Bullet
and get the party started with
80 classic and contemporary
cocktail & mocktail recipes.

Paperback / eBook

Printed in Germany
by Amazon Distribution
GmbH, Leipzig